CCE-FDPA

Comptroller of the Currency
Administrator of National Banks

I0448463

Flood Disaster Protection

Comptroller's Handbook

May 1999

CCE

Consumer Compliance Examination

Flood Disaster Protection   Table of Contents

Background

The National Flood Insurance Program (NFIP), the insurance fund that insures borrowers against the risk of loss from flooding, is administered under three statutes: the National Flood Insurance Act of 1968 (1968 Act), the Flood Disaster Protection Act of 1973 (FDPA), and Title V of the Riegle Community Development and Regulatory Improvement Act of 1994 (Title V).[1] The 1968 act made federally subsidized flood insurance available to owners of improved real estate or mobile homes located in special flood hazard areas (SFHA) if their communities participate in the NFIP. The FDPA required the federal financial regulatory agencies[2] to adopt regulations prohibiting their regulated lending institutions from making, increasing, extending or renewing a loan secured by improved real estate or a mobile home located or to be located in an SFHA in a community participating in the NFIP, unless the property securing the loan was covered by flood insurance.

Following a series of storms and high disaster relief payments by the NFIP, Title V was enacted to provide additional funding to the National Flood Insurance Fund by improving compliance with flood insurance requirements. Increased compliance and participation in the NFIP also serves to decrease the financial burden resulting from flood disasters on the federal government, taxpayers and flood victims.

Title V required the federal financial regulatory agencies to revise their flood insurance regulations to reflect the additional requirements set forth by the act. The agencies published these revisions in a joint final rule on August 29, 1996.[3] Title V also applies flood insurance requirements to loans purchased by government sponsored enterprises. Such enterprises include the Federal National Mortgage Association and the Federal Home Loan Mortgage Corporation and loans subsidized, insured or guaranteed by federal agency lenders such as the Small Business Administration, the Federal Housing Administration, and the Department of Veterans Affairs.

---

[1] These statutes are codified at 42 USC 4001-4129.

[2] The agencies are the Office of the Comptroller of the Currency (OCC), the Federal Deposit Insurance Corporation (FDIC), the Office of Thrift Supervision (OTS), the National Credit Union Administration (NCUA) and the Board of Governors of the Federal Reserve System (FRB).

[3] The OCC's implementing regulation is 12 CFR 22.

The Federal Insurance Administration (FIA), a department of the Federal Emergency Management Agency (FEMA) administers the NFIP. Its role is to:

- Make flood insurance available through the NFIP "Write Your Own" Program, which enables the public to purchase NFIP coverage from private companies that have entered into an arrangement with the FIA.

- Assist communities in adopting floodplain management.

- Administer the insurance program. Licensed property and casualty insurance agents and brokers provide the primary connection between the NFIP and the insured party. Licensed agents sell flood insurance, complete the insured party's application form, report claims, and follow-up with the insured for renewal of the policy.

Community Participation

FEMA conducts studies to determine flood hazard areas in communities in the United States. Based on these studies, FEMA issues Flood Hazard Boundary Maps and Flood Insurance Rate Maps showing the location of these areas and notifies each community of its determinations. Following notification, a community establishes its eligibility to participate in the NFIP by adopting and enforcing floodplain management ordinances that provide standards for flood damage prevention in areas susceptible to flooding. Property owners in this community then become eligible to purchase NFIP insurance for most improved real estate.

A participating community that fails to adequately enforce its floodplain management ordinances may be placed on probation by the NFIP. Policyholders in that community are notified of the probation and informed that the premiums on their NFIP policies are subject to a surcharge. If a community fails to bring its floodplain management program into compliance with NFIP requirements, the community may be suspended from the NFIP, thereby terminating its status as a participating community. In that event, NFIP policies would not be renewed for property owners in that community, no new policies would be issued, and federal disaster assistance would be limited.

Emergency Program and Regular Program

- The emergency program is an interim program that provides lower amounts of flood insurance coverage on eligible structures at subsidized rates. It is typically the first phase under which a community participates in the NFIP. The applicable map under this program is the Flood Hazard Boundary Map which designates approximate boundaries of the flood, mudslide and related erosion areas with special hazards.

- The regular program provides full insurance coverage for eligible structures and requires additional floodplain management responsibilities for the community. A community is eligible to convert to the regular program once a detailed study has been completed and a Flood Insurance Rate Map for the area has been issued. The official Flood Insurance Rate Map for a regular program community delineates both the SFHAs and the applicable risk premium zones.

Eligibility for Flood Insurance

Flood insurance is available under the NFIP on improved real property or mobile homes either located or to be located in areas identified by FEMA as having special flood hazards in participating communities. SFHAs are represented on flood maps by darkly shaded areas and have a 1 percent or greater chance of being flooded in any given year. Flood insurance coverage is also available for personal property and other insurable contents contained in real property or a mobile home located in an SFHA.

Structures Eligible for Coverage:

- Residential, industrial, commercial, and agricultural buildings that are walled and roofed structures.

- Buildings under construction for which a development loan is made to construct insurable improvements on the land. Insurance must be purchased to keep pace with the new construction.

- Mobile homes that are affixed to a permanent site, including mobile homes that are part of a dealer's inventory and affixed to permanent foundations.

- Condominiums.

- Cooperative buildings.

Structures Not Eligible for Coverage:

- Mobile homes not affixed to a permanent site.

- Buildings entirely in, on, or over water into which boats are floated.

- Buildings newly constructed or substantially improved on or after October 1, 1983, located in an area designated as an undeveloped coastal barrier with the Coastal Barrier Resources System established by the Coastal Barrier Resources Act of 1982 (16 USC 3501).

Basic Requirements

Flood insurance is required for the term of a loan when all of these factors are present:

- The financial institution makes, increases, extends, or renews any loan (commercial or consumer) secured by improved real estate or a mobile home that is or will be affixed to a permanent foundation; and

- The improved property securing the loan is located or will be located in an SFHA as identified by FEMA; and

- The community in which the improved property is located or to be located participates in the NFIP.

Loans with these three factors present are considered designated loans. Flood insurance requirements apply to designated loans even when the security interest in improved real property represents excess collateral (i.e., out of an abundance of caution). The requirements also apply to loans secured only by the improved real estate or mobile home and not secured by the land on which they are affixed.

Although a lender may make, increase, extend or renew a conventional loan in a nonparticipating community, a lender is still required to determine whether the security property is located in an SFHA and, if so, to notify the borrower. The lender must also notify the borrower that flood insurance coverage under the NFIP is not available because the community does not participate in the NFIP. If the nonparticipating community has been identified for at least one year as containing a special flood hazard area, properties located in the community will not be eligible for federal disaster relief assistance in the event of a federally-declared disaster.

Because of the lack of NFIP flood insurance coverage and limited federal disaster assistance available, a lender should carefully evaluate the risk involved in making such a loan. A lender making a loan in a nonparticipating community may want to require the purchase of private flood insurance, if available. Also, a lender with significant lending in nonparticipating communities should establish procedures to ensure that such loans do not constitute an unacceptably large portion of the financial institution's loan portfolio.

Federal agency lenders such as the Federal Housing Administration, the Small Business Administration and the Department of Veterans Affairs will not subsidize, insure, or guarantee any loan if the property securing the loan is in an SFHA of a community not participating in the NFIP. In addition, it is important for lenders to know that the Federal National Mortgage Association and the Federal Home Loan Mortgage Corporation will not purchase mortgages secured by improved properties located in SFHAs in nonparticipating communities.

Although the mandatory purchase requirements apply only to properties located in SFHAs of participating communities, NFIP flood insurance is available in all areas of participating communities. Lenders and property owners may want to exercise additional caution in areas subject to flooding, but where no flood hazards have been designated by FEMA. To facilitate the purchase of flood insurance outside SFHAs, the NFIP offers a low-cost "preferred risk" policy for structures located in zones B, C, or X. These zones are within the floodplain, but are not in SFHAs and, therefore, flood insurance is not required by law, but is recommended.

Exemptions to the Purchase Requirement

The flood insurance purchase requirement does not apply to:

- Loans on state-owned property covered by a policy of self-insurance satisfactory to the director of FEMA. FEMA publishes and periodically revises the list of states with adequate self-insurance programs. This exemption does not apply to county- or city-owned property.

- Loans with an original principal balance of $5,000 or less, and an original repayment term of one year or less.

Amount of Flood Insurance Required

The amount of flood insurance required must be at least equal to the outstanding principal balance of the loan or the maximum amount available under the NFIP, whichever is less. Mandatory purchase requirements apply only to the buildings and mobile homes that secure the loan, not to the land upon which the improvements are built. Flood insurance coverage under the NFIP is thus limited to the overall value of the property, less the value of the land. To determine the appropriate flood insurance coverage amount on a structure, lenders are advised to follow the same practices used in determining the appropriate amount of hazard insurance coverage.

When both improved real property and its contents are used to secure a designated loan, flood insurance is required for both the contents and the structure. This situation typically applies to commercial loans. Since residential mortgages rarely include personal property as collateral, borrowers are generally not required to purchase contents coverage. However, lenders are encouraged to advise borrowers to include contents coverage when it is prudent to do so.

Any changes to the current amounts of coverage available will be published in the Federal Register. The current limits of coverage, which became effective March 1, 1995, are:

Building Coverage	Emergency Program	Regular Program
Single-family dwelling	$ 35,000	$250,000
2-4 family dwelling	$ 35,000	$250,000
Other residential	$100,000	$250,000
Nonresidential	$100,000	$500,000
Contents Coverage		
Residential	$ 10,000	$100,000
Nonresidential	$100,000	$500,000

Second Mortgages/Home Equity Loans

Since only one NFIP policy can be issued on a structure, a subordinate lienholder must coordinate coverage through its borrower and the insurance agent of record. A junior lienholder's interest is established by issuing an endorsement to the existing flood insurance policy. The junior lienholder should ensure that its interest is protected by having its name appear on the policy or by other appropriate means. If a junior lienholder determines that a first mortgagee has not required sufficient coverage based on the total amount of liens on the collateral, the junior lienholder must protect its priority as to insurance proceeds by requiring the borrower to buy additional coverage. The amount required should be the lesser of all outstanding loan amounts, the value of the improved structure, or the maximum amount available.

For home equity lines of credit (HELC), it may be difficult to calculate the amount of insurance for the line since the borrower will be drawing down differing amounts on the line at different times. A bank may take one of two approaches to comply with purchase requirements for HELCs:

- Review HELC records periodically (at least annually) so that, as draws are made against the line or repayments are made to the account, the appropriate amount of flood insurance coverage can be maintained; or

- Upon origination, require the purchase of flood insurance based on the total amount of the line, the value of the improved property or the maximum amount of flood insurance coverage available, whichever is less.

Residential Condominium Policies

The condominium association of a residential building located in an SFHA may purchase NFIP insurance coverage under the Residential Condominium Building Association Policy (RCBAP). Under an RCBAP, the entire building is covered under one policy. Since the RCBAP provides flood insurance coverage for both the unit and the common property, the security interests of individual unit owners should be protected so long as adequate coverage is maintained. The maximum amount of building coverage that can be purchased is 80 percent of the replacement cost of the building or the total number of units in the condominium building times $250,000 (the maximum amount available), whichever is less. The maximum allowable contents coverage is the actual cash value of the commonly-owned contents up to a maximum of $100,000 per building.

The RCBAP does not protect an individual owner from loss to personal property owned exclusively by the unit owner. Personal property owned by an individual unit owner must be insured separately under an individual unit owner's dwelling policy. The maximum allowable contents coverage for individual residential unit owners is the actual cash value of the contents up to a maximum of $100,000.

If the condominium association has not purchased sufficient coverage under the RCBAP, the lender may request the borrower to ask the association to carry adequate coverage amounts or the lender may require the purchase of an individual residential condominium unit owner's dwelling policy.

Non-residential condominium buildings are not eligible for coverage under the RCBAP. The NFIP offers a maximum amount of building coverage up to $500,000 for these buildings and $500,000 for commonly-owned contents. The maximum allowable contents coverage for non-residential unit owners is the actual cash value of the contents up to a maximum of $500,000.

Cooperative Associations

The NFIP offers coverage for residential cooperatives with a maximum amount of building coverage up to $250,000. A cooperative cannot be insured under the RCBAP.

Timeshares

NFIP coverage of timeshares is directly related to the jurisdiction's property ownership rights, as influenced by state law. The jurisdictions generally can be divided into two categories:

- Fee or real-estate ownership, or

- Non-fee interest, such as right-to-use.

Typically, a fee or real-estate ownership timeshare that is a condominium meets the requirements for coverage under the RCBAP. The maximum amount of flood insurance available is 80 percent of the replacement cost of the building or the total number of units in the residential timeshare building times $250,000, whichever is less.

A non-fee form of ownership is similar to a cooperative where no deed is held by the unit owner and the maximum amount of insurance available is $250,000 for the building.

Multiple Structures

Each structure that secures a designated loan must be covered by flood insurance, even though the value of one structure may be sufficient to cover the loan amount. For example, assume a loan is made for $50,000 and three buildings located in SFHAs are used as collateral. Building A is valued at $50,000, Building B is $20,000 and Building C is $10,000. To comply with the mandatory flood insurance requirements, each building is required to have flood insurance. The minimum amount of insurance required would be a total of $50,000, spread among the three buildings.

FEMA does permit borrowers to insure buildings using one policy with a separate schedule that lists each building. Typically, flood insurance policies for agricultural properties and improvements are structured in this manner because they often have several buildings located on the property.

Other Real Estate Owned

An institution with other real estate owned in flood hazard areas should, as a prudent practice, purchase flood insurance policies on these properties, although it is not required to do so by the regulation.

Forced Placement Requirements

Title V of the Riegle Community Development and Regulatory Improvement Act of 1994 requires lenders or servicers to force place flood insurance if they determine at any time during the life of the loan that the security property is not adequately insured. The first step in the forced placement procedures requires the lender or servicer to notify the borrower of the need to carry an adequate amount of flood insurance coverage. Although the act does not specify the precise wording of this notice, it must state that:

- The borrower should, at the borrower's expense, obtain flood insurance that is not less than the minimum amount required under the law.

- The borrower has 45 days to purchase the insurance.

- If the borrower does not show evidence of obtaining such coverage within 45 days after notification, the lender or servicer will purchase the insurance on behalf of the borrower and may charge the borrower for the cost of premiums and fees incurred in purchasing the insurance.

If, after 45 days from the notice, the borrower fails to obtain flood insurance coverage, a lender or servicer must obtain an NFIP policy through a "Write Your Own" insurer that participates in the Mortgage Portfolio Protection Program or from a private industry insurer.

FEMA has developed the Mortgage Portfolio Protection Program to assist lenders in connection with forced placement procedures. When flood insurance is involuntarily placed, many loans must be processed with a limited amount of underwriting information. Therefore, placement through this program is appropriate when only limited underwriting information is obtained.

The amount that must be forced placed is equal to the difference between the present amount of coverage and the lesser of the outstanding principal balance, the value of the improved property, or the maximum coverage limit. Forced placement is not appropriate when an institution makes, increases, extends, or renews a loan, because flood insurance coverage is required prior to closing.

Standard Flood Hazard Determination Form

When an institution makes, increases, extends, or renews any commercial or consumer loan secured by improved real estate or by a mobile home, it must use the Standard Flood Hazard Determination Form (SFHDF) developed by FEMA to determine whether the building or mobile home offered as security is or will be located in an SFHA. The lender may choose to have the form completed internally or may use an outside service to make the flood hazard determination and complete the SFHDF.

A financial institution can use a printed, computerized, or electronic form so long as it contains the mandatory fields indicated on the SFHDF. It must keep a copy of the completed form, either in hard copy or electronic format, for the period of time it owns the loan. The form does not need to be kept in the loan file, but a lender is expected to be able to retrieve the record within a reasonable time period.

Use of this form became mandatory on January 2, 1996; the form was revised in October, 1998. A sample SFHDF can be found in appendix B.

Reliance on Prior Determination

An institution may rely on a previous determination when it increases, extends, renews, or purchases a loan. Prior determinations may not be used when a bank makes a loan. However, subsequent transactions by the same institution with respect to the same property, such as assumptions, refinancings and junior lien loans, are considered renewals. A new determination would not be required in those circumstances, assuming the following conditions are met:

- The previous determination is not more than seven years old; and

- No new or revised flood map has been issued in the interim; and

- The determination was recorded on the SFHDF.

Review of Determinations

Letter of Map Amendment (LOMA)

A flood map will occasionally show a property as being in an SFHA, even though the building on the property is actually above the base flood elevation. In practice, flood insurance maps do not reflect every rise in terrain, and there may be instances of high ground inadvertently included in the SFHAs. Nevertheless, lenders are bound by the information shown on FEMA maps until the map is changed by FEMA.

To resolve such a situation, a property owner can submit elevation materials with a request to FEMA for a LOMA to remove the property from the SFHA. The request must be submitted on FEMA Form 81-92, "Application Form for Single Residential Lot or Structures – Amendments and Revisions to the National Flood Insurance Program Maps" (1/97). The form may be obtained from FEMA's Web site (www.fema.gov/library/MT-EZ.pdf), from FEMA's fax-on-demand line, or by calling a FEMA Regional Office (see appendix D).

To obtain the information to complete the form, it may be necessary for a borrower to hire a qualified, licensed surveyor. FEMA has up to 60 days to respond. After obtaining a LOMA, a borrower must submit it to the lender for the flood insurance requirement to be waived. The lender has the discretion to continue to require flood insurance if the lender determines it is prudent to do so.

Letter of Map Revision (LOMR) – Based on Fill

A LOMR is appropriate when physical changes are necessary to raise the land above the base flood elevation 100-year flood level. For example, a LOMR request is appropriate when a property, located within an SFHA, is graded and filled to raise the level of the land above the base flood elevation 100 - year flood level. The request for a LOMR must be initiated and approved by the community since changes in land level may affect other property owners. Community approval also confirms that the change in the land has been reviewed and is compatible with the community's planning.

A LOMR request must be submitted to FEMA on the same form as the LOMA (see above description of Form 81-92) and is available on FEMA's Web site www.fema.gov/library/MT-EZ.pdf, from FEMA's fax-on-demand line, or by calling a FEMA Regional Office (see appendix D).

FEMA has up to 90 days to respond to a LOMR request. After obtaining a LOMR, the borrower must submit it to the lender before the flood insurance requirement can be waived. The lender has the discretion to continue to require flood insurance if the lender determines that it is prudent to do so.

Letter of Determination Review (LODR) – Contested Determination

A LODR is used to resolve a disagreement between the borrower and the lender with the SFHA determination. When a borrower contests a lender's determination that a property is located in an SFHA and that flood insurance is required, the borrower and lender may jointly submit a request to FEMA to review the determination. The request must be submitted within 45 days after the borrower is notified that flood insurance is required. Flood insurance is required during this 45-day processing period.

The determination review process requires both parties to present technical information to FEMA. This information includes the completed Standard Flood Hazard Determination Form, a copy of the lender's notification to the borrower, applicable NFIP map panels and all other technical information used in making the flood hazard determination.

The request for a determination review must be signed by the lender and at least one of the borrowers. FEMA will not accept the signature of a third-party determinator as a representative for either the borrower or the lender.

Determination Fees

An institution or its servicer may charge the borrower a reasonable fee for the cost of making a flood hazard determination under the following circumstances:

- The borrower initiates a transaction (making, increasing, extending, or renewing a loan) that triggers a flood hazard determination;

- FEMA has revised or updated the flood maps for that area; or

- The determination results in the purchase of flood insurance under the forced placement provision.

Banks may also charge a borrower a reasonable fee for life-of-loan service, which monitors the flood hazard status of the secured property for the term of the loan, by the bank, by its servicer, or by a third party, such as a flood hazard determination company.

Truth in Lending Act Issues

The Official Staff Commentary to Regulation Z (12 CFR 226.4(c)(7)-3) states that a fee for services that will be performed periodically during the term of a loan is a finance charge, regardless of whether the fee is imposed at closing, or when the service is performed. This would include a fee for life-of-loan service to monitor the flood hazard status of the secured property for the term of the loan. However, a fee for the initial determination of whether a security property is in an SFHA is excluded from the finance charge. The commentary further advises that any portion of a fee that does not relate to the initial decision to grant credit must be included in the finance charge.[4] If creditors are uncertain about what portion of a fee is related to the initial decision to grant credit, the entire fee may be treated as a finance charge.

Escrow Requirements

The escrow provisions are designed to improve compliance with flood insurance requirements by ensuring that homeowners whose properties are located in SFHAs obtain and maintain flood insurance for the life of the loan. The escrowing of flood insurance premiums is mandatory when a lender requires the borrower to escrow for other funds associated with the loan, such as taxes, insurance premiums or any other fees or charges. Voluntary payments for credit life insurance do not trigger the escrow requirement for flood insurance premiums.

The escrow requirement is limited to loans secured by "residential improved real estate." Title V defines "residential improved real estate" as "improved real estate for which the improvement is a residential building." Therefore, the determining factor in applying the escrow requirement is not the purpose of the loan, but the purpose of the building. For example, the escrow provision covers residential rental properties and multifamily properties containing five or more residential units.

---

[4] See 12 CFR part 226, supplement 1, comment 4(c)(7)-3.

Notice Requirements

When the secured property for a loan is or will be located in an SFHA, regardless of whether the security property is located in a participating or nonparticipating community, the lender must provide a written notice to the borrower and the servicer. The written notice must contain the following information:

- A warning that the building or mobile home is or will be located in an SFHA.

- A description of the flood insurance purchase requirements.

- A statement, where applicable, that flood insurance coverage is available under the NFIP and may also be available from private insurers.

- A statement noting whether federal disaster relief assistance may be available in the event of damage to the building or mobile home, caused by flooding in a federally declared disaster.

Delivery of the notice must take place within a reasonable time before the transaction is completed. The agencies generally regard ten days prior to closing as a reasonable time interval. However, what constitutes a reasonable time will vary according to the circumstances of particular transactions.

A lender may use the sample form provided in 12 CFR 22, appendix A. Use of the sample form is optional. A lender may personalize and change the format of the sample form, but must provide the borrower with the minimum information required by the regulation.

Notice to Servicer

Loan servicers must also be notified of special flood hazards. Since a servicer's identity may not be known until after a loan closing, advance notification may not be possible. However, the notice to the servicer should be provided as promptly as practicable after the financial institution gives notice to the borrower. Notice to the servicer must be given no later than when the lender transmits other loan data to the servicer concerning hazard insurance and taxes. Delivery to the servicer of a copy of the borrower's notice suffices as notice to the servicer.

Notice to the Director of FEMA

A lender must notify the director of FEMA, or the director's designee, of the identity of the loan servicer and of any change in the servicer. FEMA has designated the insurance carrier as its designee for this purpose. Notice of the identity of the servicer will enable the insurance carrier to notify the loan servicer 45 days before a flood insurance policy expires. Also, a notice of any change in the loan servicer must be sent to the insurance carrier within 60 days of the effective date of a servicing transfer. Although no standard notice form is required, the information provided should be sufficient to identify the security property and the loan, as well as the new servicer and the servicer's address.

Record Keeping Requirements

The record keeping requirements include retention of:

- Copies of completed SFHD forms, in either hard copy or electronic form, for as long as the bank owns the loan; and

- Records of receipt of notices to the borrower and the servicer for as long as the bank owns the loan.

Although there is no particular form, the record of receipt should contain a statement from the borrower indicating that the borrower has received the notification. Examples of records of receipt may include a borrower's signed acknowledgment on a copy of the notice, a borrower-initialed list of documents and disclosures that the lender provided the borrower, or a scanned electronic image of a receipt or other document signed by the borrower.

A lender may keep the record of receipt provided by the borrower and the servicer in the form that best suits the bank's business practices. Lenders who retain these records electronically must be able to retrieve them within a reasonable time.

Penalties and Liabilities

There are penalties when a lender fails to place insurance, escrow flood insurance policy premiums on applicable loans, provide notice requirements on applicable loans or, if necessary, force place flood insurance on designated loans. If a lender is found to have a pattern or practice of committing violations, the OCC will consider assessing civil penalties in an amount not to exceed $350 per violation with a total amount against any one bank not to exceed $100,000 in any calendar year. Any penalty assessed will be paid into the National Flood Mitigation Fund. Liability for violations cannot be transferred to a subsequent purchaser of a loan. No penalties can be imposed four years after the date of the occurrence of the violation.

General Procedures

Objective: Determine the scope of the examination for compliance with the Flood Disaster Protection Act (FDPA).

1. From the examiner assigned the Compliance Management System program, obtain and review the following documents to identify any previous problems that require follow-up:

    - ☐ Historical examination findings.
    - ☐ Complaint information.
    - ☐ Internal and external audit reports, including any management assertions.
    - ☐ Minutes of any audit committees, and applicable board of director minutes since the last examination.
    - ☐ Significant findings from compliance audit.
    - ☐ Working papers from the prior examination.

2. Determine during early discussions with management:

    - Management supervision of FDPA compliance.
    - Types of products or services offered.
    - Volume of products or transactions.
    - Bank's locations and markets.
    - Changes in processes, including forms, contracts, software programs, etc.
    - Significant changes in policies, personnel, or controls.
    - Internal or external factors that could affect FDPA compliance.

3. Complete the "Quality of Risk Management" procedures.

4. Complete all or a portion of the "Quantity of Risk" procedures. The procedures performed in the "Quantity of Risk" section should address areas where the bank's compliance management system is deficient as identified during the "Quality of Risk Management" review.

Quality of Risk Management

Conclusion: The quality of risk management is (strong, satisfactory, weak).

Policy

Conclusion: The board (has/has not) established appropriate policies to ensure compliance with the FDPA.

Objective: Determine whether the bank has appropriate formal/informal policies to ensure compliance with the FDPA.

1. Determine whether the board has adopted and management has implemented adequate policies and procedures to maintain compliance with the FDPA. Where appropriate, they should address:

    - Significant requirements of the regulation.
    - Responsibilities and accountabilities for key personnel.
    - Training program.
    - Process for responding to changes in laws and regulations.
    - Role of audit and compliance review.

2. Determine whether the board or an appropriate committee periodically reviews and approves compliance policies.

Processes

Conclusion: Management (has/has not) established effective processes to ensure compliance with the FDPA.

Objective: Determine whether reliance can be placed on the bank's processes to prevent violations of the FDPA.

1. Determine whether the bank's system for communicating the requirements of, and any subsequent changes to, consumer protection laws and regulations is adequate to ensure ongoing compliance.

2. Review the following documents and discuss with management to determine whether internal controls are adequate to ensure compliance with the FDPA. Identify procedures used daily to prevent errors and violations and ensure data integrity.

    - Organizational charts.
    - Process flowcharts.

- Policies and procedures.
- Loan documentation and disclosures.
- Checklists, worksheets, and review documents.
- Computer programs, if applicable.

3. Assess the procedures used to ensure compliance when new products are developed and operational changes occur (e.g., flood hazard determination form, determination fees, servicers, servicer fees, and software programs).

Personnel

Conclusion: Bank management and personnel (do/do not) possess the required technical skills and knowledge to ensure compliance with the FDPA.

Objective: Determine whether bank management and personnel possess sufficient knowledge and technical skills to manage and perform duties related to the FDPA.

1. Assess bank management and personnel's knowledge and technical skills regarding the FDPA based on conclusions developed while performing these procedures. Also consider:

- Employee roles and responsibilities.
- Training and experience.
- Violations cited.

2. Review the bank's training program (materials, agendas, rosters, frequency, evaluation forms, etc.) and discuss with management to determine how frequently and how well employees throughout the bank (private banking, fiduciary, international, etc.) are trained regarding compliance with laws and regulations.

Controls

Conclusion: Management (has/has not) established effective control systems to ensure compliance with the FDPA.

Objective: Determine whether reliance can be placed on the bank's control systems to detect and correct violations of the FDPA, including practices and procedures performed by audit and compliance review.

1. Review audit/compliance review working papers to determine whether:

- Procedures used address all regulatory provisions (see Quantity of Risk section).

- Steps are taken to follow-up on previously identified deficiencies.
- Procedures used include samples that cover all product types and decision centers.
- Work performed is accurate (through a review of some transactions).
- Significant deficiencies, and the root cause of the deficiencies, are included in reports to management and the board.
- Corrective actions are timely and appropriate.
- The area is reviewed at an appropriate interval.

2. Review the following documents and discuss with management to determine whether management information systems are sufficient and whether adequate practices are in place to ensure that timely and appropriate corrective action is taken when weaknesses/violations are identified or when consumer complaints indicate significant deficiencies.

   - Audit/compliance review policies, procedures, and working papers.
   - Audit/compliance review reports and management responses.
   - Management reports.

Quantity of Risk

Conclusion: The quantity of risk is (low, moderate, high).

Objective: Determine the bank's level of compliance with the Flood Disaster Protection Act (FDPA).

1. Review a sample of loan files to verify that the bank's policies are followed and assess the bank's level of compliance by completing the FDPA worksheet in appendix A.

   - The sample should include commercial and consumer loans secured by improved real property or mobile homes. A portion of the loans should be secured by improved property or a mobile home located or to be located in an SFHA in a participating community.

2. If the bank has failed to maintain adequate flood insurance coverage on designated loans, require the bank to review its loan portfolio to determine the extent of the problem. Instruct the bank to obtain the necessary flood insurance coverage on those loans lacking adequate coverage.

   - The bank has the duty and the authority to force place insurance. If, at any time during the life of a covered loan, the lender or servicer determines that the property securing the loan is not covered, or not adequately covered by flood insurance, the lender must notify the borrower of the need to obtain flood insurance coverage. The notice must state that the borrower should, at the borrower's expense, obtain flood insurance coverage in an amount that is at least equal to the amount required under the law. If the borrower fails to purchase such flood insurance within 45 days after notification, the lender or servicer shall purchase the insurance on behalf of the borrower and may charge the borrower for the cost of premiums and fees incurred by the lender or servicer. (12 CFR 22.7).

Conclusions

Objective: Prepare written conclusion summaries, discuss findings with EIC, and communicate findings to management. If necessary, initiate corrective action when policies or internal controls are deficient or when violations of law or regulation are identified.

1. Summarize findings and violations from the worksheet and the preceding procedural steps to assess the bank's level of compliance with the requirements of the FDPA.

2. For those violations found to be significant or a pattern or practice, determine the root cause of violation(s) by identifying weaknesses in:

   - Internal controls.
   - Audit/independent compliance review.
   - Training.
   - Management oversight.
   - Other factors.

3. Form a conclusion about the reliability of the compliance management system for the FDPA, and provide conclusions to the examiner performing the Compliance Management System program.

4. Identify action needed to correct violations and weaknesses in the bank's compliance system, as appropriate.

5. Determine whether civil money penalties (CMP) or an enforcement action should be recommended (refer to 42 USC 4012a(f)).

6. Determine whether any items identified during this examination could develop into supervisory concerns before the next on-site examination (considering whether the bank has plans to increase monitoring in the affected area, or anticipates changes in personnel, policy, outside auditors or consultants, or business strategy). If so, summarize your concerns and assess the potential risk to the bank.

7. Determine the impact on the aggregate and the direction of risk assessment for any concerns identified during the review. Examiners should refer to guidance provided under the OCC's large and community bank risk assessment programs.

   - Risk Categories: Compliance, Transaction, Reputation.
   - Risk Conclusions: High, Moderate, or Low.
   - Risk Direction: Increasing, Stable, or Declining.

8. Provide, and discuss with, the EIC (and the supervisory office, if appropriate) conclusions, including:

    - Summary of violations and recommended CMPs/enforcement actions, if any.
    - Recommended corrective action.
    - Quality of risk management and quantity of risk.
    - Recommended Matters Requiring Board Attention (MRBA).
    - MRBA comments should cover practices that:
        - Deviate from sound fundamental principles and are likely to result in financial deterioration if not addressed.
        - Result in substantive noncompliance with laws.
    - MRBA should discuss:
        - Causative factors contributing to the problem.
        - Consequences of inaction.
        - Management's commitment to corrective action.
        - The time frame and person(s) responsible for corrective action.

9. Discuss findings with management. Obtain commitment(s) for corrective action as needed. Include in the discussion:

    - Quality of risk management.
    - Quantity of risk (include a listing of all violations, as well as significant violations).
    - MRBA(s).

10. As appropriate, prepare a brief comment for inclusion in the report of examination.

11. Prepare a memorandum summarizing work performed (e.g., sampling method used, internal control systems, scope of audit review, conclusions regarding audit, etc.) and update the work program with any information that will facilitate future examinations. Update the OCC database on all violations of law or regulation.

12. Organize and reference working papers in accordance with OCC guidance (PPM 5400-8).

FDPA Worksheet

This worksheet is used in conjunction with the examination procedures. Also, it is offered as a tool for compliance auditors reviewing loans subject to flood insurance requirements. The worksheet is designed as a decision tree that will guide the user through the requirements of the FDPA.

To use the worksheet, select a sample of commercial and consumer loans secured by improved real estate or a mobile home.

Note: Loans not requiring the purchase of flood insurance include those:

- Secured by state-owned property subject to an acceptable self-insurance policy; or

- With an original principal balance of $5,000 or less and a repayment term of one year or less.

Name of Borrower: Loan #					

If the loan was made, increased, extended, or renewed before ½/96, skip to step 2. Otherwise:
 	
1.   Was the Standard Flood Hazard Determination Form prepared?
 	
     If NO, cite violation of §22.6(a).
 	
1a.   Did the bank retain a copy of the completed Standard Flood Hazard Determination form for this loan?
 	
     If NO, cite violation of §22.6(b).					

2.   Is the improved property or mobile home located or to be located in an SFHA?
 	
     If NO, skip to step 7.
 	
2a.   Is the improved property or mobile home located or to be located in a participating community?
 	
     If YES, skip to step 3.
 	
2b.   Is the loan insured or guaranteed by a government agency (e.g., SBA, FHA, VA, etc.)?
 	
     If NO, skip to step 7.
 	
     If YES, a referral must be made to the appropriate government agency (e.g., SBA, VA, FHA). See 42 USC 4106(a). Perform step 3 and then skip to step 7.					

3.   Did the bank give the borrower and servicer, if applicable, notice that the improved property or mobile home securing the loan is located or will be located in an SFHA?
 	
     If NO, cite a violation of §22.9(a) and skip to step 4.
 	
3a.   Did the notice include the required information?
 	
     If NO, cite a violation of §22.9(b).
 	
3b.   Did the bank provide the notice to the borrower within a reasonable time prior to closing?
 	
     If NO, cite a violation of §22.9(c).
 	
3c.   If applicable, after providing the notice to the borrower, did the bank provide notice to the servicer as promptly as practicable?
 	
     If NO, cite a violation of §22.9(c).
 	
3d.   Did the bank retain a record of receipt of the notices by the borrower and the servicer?
 	
     If NO, cite a violation of §22.9(d).					

Name of Borrower: Loan #					
4. Is the loan covered by an adequate amount of flood insurance? If YES, skip to step 5. **4a.** Has the loan been uninsured or underinsured longer than 45 calendar days? If YES, cite a violation of §22.3(a) and skip to step 5. **4b.** Did the bank send a notice requesting that the borrower purchase flood insurance within 45 calendar days or the bank would force place the insurance? If NO, cite a violation of §22.7.					
5. If the loan closed after 10/1/96, does the improved property or mobile home meet the definition of residential improved real estate per §22.2(l)? If NO, skip to step 6. **5a.** Does the bank require the borrower to escrow taxes, insurance premiums, fees or any other charges? If NO, skip to step 6. **5b.** Are flood insurance premiums escrowed? If NO, cite violation of §22.5.					
6. If the bank made, increased, extended, renewed, sold, or transferred the loan, did the bank notify the insurance carrier in writing of the loan servicer's identity? If NO, cite violation of §22.10 (a) and skip to step 7. **6a.** If servicing was sold or transferred, did the bank notify the insurance carrier within 60 days after the effective date of the change? If NO, cite violation of §22.10(b).					
7. Were the fees charged to borrowers for flood determinations (including life of loan monitoring service) reasonable? If NO, cite violation of §22.8(a). **7a.** Were the determination fees charged under permissible circumstances? If NO, cite violation of §22.8(b)(1), (2), (3) or (4).					

Standard Flood Hazard Determination Form

When a bank makes, increases, extends, or renews a loan secured by improved real estate or by a mobile home, it must use the Standard Flood Hazard Determination Form (SFHDF) to determine whether the building or mobile home offered as security property is or will be located in an SFHA.

The form may be used in printed, computerized or electronic format so long as it contains all the mandatory fields. The following page is a copy of the revised Standard Flood Hazard Determination Form (FEMA Form 81-93). The revised form became effective in October 1998 and has an expiration date of October 31, 2001. The form may be locally reproduced from the attached copy. The form may also be obtained through FEMA's fax-on-demand at 202-646-FEMA, request document #23103 or by mail from the FEMA publication office at 800-480-2520 or on FEMA's Web site at www.fema.gov/library/sfldfrm.pdf.

STANDARD FLOOD HAZARD DETERMINATION

See The Attached Instructions

O.M.B. No. 3067-0264 Expires October 31, 2001

SECTION I - LOAN INFORMATION

1. LENDER NAME AND ADDRESS

2. COLLATERAL *(Building/Mobile Home/Personal Property)* PROPERTY ADDRESS *(Legal Description may be attached)*

3. LENDER ID. NO.

4. LOAN IDENTIFIER

5. AMOUNT OF FLOOD INSURANCE REQUIRED
$

SECTION II

A. NATIONAL FLOOD INSURANCE PROGRAM (NFIP) COMMUNITY JURISDICTION

1. NFIP Community Name	2. County(ies)	3. State	4. NFIP Community Number

B. NATIONAL FLOOD INSURANCE PROGRAM (NFIP) DATA AFFECTING BUILDING/MOBILE HOME

1. NFIP Map Number or Community-Panel Number (Community name, if not the same as "A")	2. NFIP Map Panel Effective/ Revised Date	3. LOMA/LOMR	4. Flood Zone	5. No NFIP Map
		☐ yes ___ Date		

C. FEDERAL FLOOD INSURANCE AVAILABILITY *(Check all that apply)*

1. ☐ Federal Flood insurance is available *(community participates in NFIP).* ☐ Regular Program ☐ Emergency Program of NFIP

2. ☐ Federal Flood insurance is not available because community is not participating in the NFIP.

3. ☐ Building/Mobile Home is in a Coastal Barrier Resources Area (CBRA) or Otherwise Protected Area (OPA), Federal Flood insurance may not be available.

CBRA/OPA designation date: _____

D. DETERMINATION

IS BUILDING/MOBILE HOME IN SPECIAL FLOOD HAZARD AREA (ZONES CONTAINING THE LETTERS "A" OR "V")? ☐ YES ☐ NO

If yes, flood insurance is required by the Flood Disaster Protection Act of 1973.

If no, flood insurance is not required by the Flood Disaster Protection Act of 1973.

E. COMMENTS *(Optional)*:

This determination is based on examining the NFIP map, any Federal Emergency Management Agency revisions to it, and any other information needed to locate the building/mobile home on the NFIP map.

F. PREPARER'S INFORMATION

NAME, ADDRESS, TELEPHONE NUMBER *(If other than Lender)*	DATE OF DETERMINATION

This form may be locally reproduced.

STANDARD FLOOD HAZARD DETERMINATION FORM INSTRUCTIONS
PAPERWORK BURDEN DISCLOSURE NOTICE

Public reporting burden for FEMA Form 81-93 form is estimated to average 20 minutes per response. The burden estimate includes the time for reviewing instructions, searching existing data sources, gathering and maintaining the data needed, and completing and reviewing the form. Send comments regarding the accuracy of the burden estimate and any suggestions for reducing the burden to: Information Collections Management, Federal Emergency Management Agency, 500 C Street, SW, Washington, DC 20742; and to the Office of Management and Budget, Paperwork Reduction Project (30676- 0264), Washington, DC 20503.

SECTION 1

1. **LENDER NAME**: Enter lender name and address.

2. COLLATERAL (Building/Mobile Home/Personal Property) PROPERTY ADDRESS: Enter property address for the insurable collateral. In rural areas, a postal address may not be sufficient to locate the property. In these cases, legal property descriptions may be used and may be attached to the form if space provided is insufficient.

3. LENDER ID. NO.: The lender funding the loan should identify itself as follows: FDIC-insured lenders should indicate their FDIC Insurance Certificate Number; Federally-insured credit unions should indicate their charter/insurance number; Farm Credit institutions should indicate their UNINUM number. Other lenders who fund loans sold to or securitized by FNMA or FHLMC should enter the FNMA or FHLMC seller/servicer number.

4. LOAN IDENTIFIER: Optional. May be used by lenders to conform with their individual method of identifying loans.

5. AMOUNT OF FLOOD INSURANCE REQUIRED: Optional. The minimum federal requirement for this amount is the lesser of: the outstanding principal loan balance; the value of the improved property, mobile home and/or personal property used to secure the loan; or the maximum statutory limit of flood insurance coverage. Lenders may exceed the minimum federal requirements. National Flood Insurance Program (NFIP) policies do not provide coverage in excess of the value of the building/mobile home/personal property.

SECTION 2

A. NATIONAL FLOOD INSURANCE PROGRAM (NFIP) COMMUNITY JURISDICTION

1. NFIP Community Name. Enter the complete name of the community (as indicated on the NFIP map) in which the building or mobile home is located. Under the NFIP, a community is the political unit that has authority to adopt and enforce floodplain management regulations for the areas within its jurisdiction. A community may be any State or area or political subdivision thereof, or any Indian tribe or authorized tribal organization, or Alaska Native village or authorized native organization. (Examples: Brewer, City of; Washington, Borough of; Worchester, Township of; Baldwin County; Jefferson Parish.) For a building or mobile home that may have been annexed by one community but is shown on another community's NFIP map, enter the Community Name for the community with land-use jurisdiction over the building or mobile home.

2. County(ies). Enter the name of the county or counties in which the community is located. For unicorporated areas of a county, enter "unincorporated areas". For independent cities, enter "independent city."

3. State. Enter the two-digit state abbreviation. (Examples: VA, TX, CA.)

4. NFIP Community Number. Enter the 6-digit NFIP community number. This number can be determined by consulting the NFIP Community Status Book or can be found on the NFIP map; copies of either can be obtained from FEMA's Website http://www.fema.gov or by calling 1-800-611-6125. If not NFIP Community Number exists for the community, enter "none".

B. NFIP DATA AFFECTING BUILDING/MOBILE HOME

The information in this section (excluding the LOMA/LOMR information) is obtained by reviewing the NFIP map on which the building/mobile home is located. The current NFIP map, and a pamphlet titled "Guide to Flood Maps," may be obtained from FEMA by calling 1-800-611-6125. Note that even when an NFIP map panel is not printed, it may be reflected on a community's NFIP map index with its proper number, date, and flood zone indicated; enter these data accordingly.

1. NFIP Map Number or Community-Panel Number. Enter the 11-digit number shown on the NFIP map that covers the building or mobile home. (Examples: 480214 0022C; 58103C0075 F.) Some older maps will have a 9-digit number (Example: 12345601A.) Note that the first six digits will not match the NFIP Community Number when the sixth digit is a "C" or when one community has annexed land from another but the NFIP map has not yet been updated to reflect this annexation. When the sixth digit is a "C", the NFIP map is in countywide format and shows the flood hazards for the geographic areas of the county on one map, including flood hazards for incorporated communities and for any unincorporated county contained within the county's geographic limits. Such countywide maps will list an NFIP Map Number. For maps not in such countywide format, the NFIP map will list a Community-Panel Number on each panel. If no NFIP map is in effect for the location of the building or mobile home, enter "none".

2. NFIP Map Panel Effective/Revised Date. Enter the map effective date or the map revised date shown on the NFIP map. (Example: 6/15/93.) this will be the latest of all dates shown on the map.

3. LOMA/LOMR. If a Letter of Map Amendment (LOMA) or Letter of Map Revision (LOMR) has been issued by FEMA since the current Map Panel Effective/Revised Date that revises the flood hazards affecting the building or mobile home, check "yes" and specify the date of the letter; otherwise, no entry is required. Information on LOMAs and LOMRs is available form the following sources:

* The community's official copy of its NFIP map should have a copy of all subsequently-issued LOMAs and LOMRs attached to it.
* For LOMAs and LOMRs issued on or after October 1, 1994, FEMA publishes a list of these letters twice a year as a compendium in the Federal Register; This information is also available on FEMA's website at http://www.fema.gov.
* A subscription service providing digitized copies of these letters on CD-ROM is also available by calling 1-800-358-9616.

4. Flood Zone. Enter the flood zone(s) covering the building or mobile home. (Examples: A, AE, A4, AR, AR/A, AR/AE, AR/AO, V, VE, V12, AH, AO, B, C, X, D.) If any part of the building or mobile home is within the Special Flood Hazard Area (SFHA), the entire building or mobile home is considered to be in the SFHA. All flood zones beginning with the letter "A" or "V" are considered Special Flood Hazard Areas (SFHAs). Each flood zone is defined in the legend of the NFIP map on which it appears. If there is no NFIP map for the subject area, enter "none."

5. No NFIP Map. If no NFIP map covers the area where the building or mobile home is located, check this box.

C. **FEDERAL FLOOD INSURANCE AVAILABILITY**. Check all boxes that apply; however, note that boxes 1 (Federal Flood Insurance is available...) and 2 (Federal Flood Insurance is not available...) are mutually exclusive. Federal flood insurance is available to all residents of a community that participates in the NFIP. Community participation status can be determined by consulting the NFIP Community Status Book, which is available from FEMA and at http://www.fema.gov. The NFIP Community Status Book will indicate whether or not the community is participating in the NFIP and whether participation is in the Emergency or Regular Program. If the community participates in the NFIP, check either Regular Program or Emergency Program. To obtain Federal flood insurance, a copy of this completed form may be provided to an insurance agent.

Federal flood insurance is prohibited in designated Coastal Barrier Resources Areas (CBRA) and Otherwise Protected Areas (OPAs) for buildings or mobile homes built or substantially improved after the date of the CBRA or OPA designation. An information sheet explaining the Coastal Barrier Resources System may be obtained from FEMA by calling 1-800-611-6125.

D. **DETERMINATION**: If any portion of the building/mobile home is in an identified Special Flood Hazard Area (SFHA), check yes (flood insurance is required). If no portion of the building/mobile home is in an identified SFHA, check no. If no NFIP map exists for the community, check no. If no NFIP map exists, Section B5 should also be checked.

F. **PREPARER'S INFORMATION**: If other than the lender, enter the name, address, and telephone number of the company or organization performing the flood hazard determination. An individual's name may be included, but is not required.

Date of Determination. Enter date on which flood hazard determination was completed.

OTHER INFORMATION

MULTIPLE BUILDINGS: If the loan collateral includes more than one building, a schedule for the additional building(s)/mobile home(s) indicating the determination for each may be attached. Otherwise, a separate form must be completed for each building or mobile home. Any attachment(s) should be noted in the comment section. A separate flood insurance policy is required for each building or mobile home.

GUARANTEES REGARDING INFORMATION: Determinations on this form made by persons other than the lender are acceptable only to the extent that the accuracy of the information is guaranteed.

FORM AVAILABILITY: Copies of this form are available from the FEMA fax-on-demand line by calling (202) 646-FEMA and requesting form #23103. Guidance on using the form in a printed, computerized, or electronic format is contained in form #23110. This information is also available on FEMA's website http://www.fema.gov.

Interagency Questions and Answers

This document answers questions about the revised flood insurance regulation commonly asked by banks and other interested parties. The document was jointly issued by the Farm Credit Administration, the Federal Deposit Insurance Corporation, the Federal Reserve Board, the National Credit Union Administration, the Office of the Comptroller of the Currency, and the Office of Thrift Supervision under the auspices of the Federal Financial Institutions Examination Council.

The document does not anticipate all circumstances or contingencies that may affect particular financial institutions. The agencies will issue further staff guidance as they gain experience in applying the revised regulation.

For ease of reference, the following terms are used throughout the document: "Act" refers to the National Flood Insurance Reform Act of 1994 (Title V of the Riegle Community Development and Regulatory Improvement Act of 1994 [Pub. L.103-325, title V, 108 Stat. 2160, 2255-87 (September 23, 1994)]). "Regulation" refers to the joint final rule adopted by the agencies. (61 Fed. Reg. 45684 (August 29, 1996)).

I.   DEFINITIONS

Designated Loan – A loan secured by a building or mobile home that is located or to be located in a special flood hazard area (SFHA) in which flood insurance is available under the act.

1. Is an interim loan to construct a commercial building included in this definition?

ANSWER: Yes. If the purpose of the loan is to construct a building (assuming the loan is secured by that building), the regulation applies. If the community where the property is located participates in the National Flood Insurance Program (NFIP), then the NFIP policy, subject to certain conditions and restrictions, can be purchased to provide coverage during the construction period for a building that will be located in an SFHA.

2. Are loans secured by raw land that will be developed into buildable lots subject to the regulation?

ANSWER: No. An acquisition and development loan would not be subject to the regulation because it does not meet the definition of a "designated loan." However, when the final construction phase of an ADC (acquisition, development, construction) project is begun, the regulation becomes effective. This will require lenders to determine whether the property is located in an SFHA. If the building securing the loan is located or to be located in an SFHA, the other requirements of the regulation will also apply. As noted above, the NFIP permits a policy (subject to certain conditions and restrictions) to be purchased prior to the actual construction of a building.

3. Is a home equity loan considered a "designated loan"?

ANSWER: Yes, a home equity (or other) loan can be a designated loan, regardless of the lien priority if: the loan is secured by a building or a mobile home; the collateral is located in an SFHA; and, the community where the property is located participates in the NFIP.

4. Is a draw against an approved line of credit a "triggering event" requiring a flood determination under the regulation or is it only the original application for the line of credit that triggers a determination?

ANSWER: Assuming that the line of credit is secured by a building and is thereby a "designated loan," a determination is required when application is made for the loan. A draw against an approved line would not require a further determination. However, a request for an increase in the line of approved credit is a triggering event and might require a new determination, depending upon whether a previous determination was done. (See the response to Question 4 in Section V, Required Use of Standard Flood Hazard Determination form.)

5. If the loan request is to finance inventory stored in a building located within an SFHA but the building is not security for the loan, is flood insurance required?

ANSWER: No. Title V of the Riegle Community Development and Regulatory Improvement Act of 1994 looks to the collateral securing the loan. In this example, the collateral does not meet the definition of a "designated loan" because it is not a building or mobile home.

6. If the building and contents both secure the loan, and the building is located in an SFHA, in a community that participates in the NFIP, what are the requirements for flood insurance? What if the contents securing the loan are located in buildings other than the building securing the loan?

ANSWER: Flood insurance is required for the building located in the SFHA and any contents stored in that building. If collateral securing the loan is stored in buildings that do not secure the loan and these buildings are not located in an SFHA, then flood insurance is not required on those contents.

7. Does the regulation apply when the lender is taking a security interest only as an "abundance of caution"?

ANSWER: Yes. Title V looks to the collateral securing the loan, not to the purpose of the loan. If the lender takes a security interest in improved real estate, the regulation applies without regard to the purpose of the loan.

8. If a borrower offers a note on a single-family dwelling as collateral for a personal loan but the lender does not take a security interest in the dwelling itself, is this a "designated loan"?

ANSWER: No. A designated loan is a loan secured by a building or mobile home. In this example, the lender did not take a security interest in the building, therefore the loan is not a "designated loan."

9. Does the regulation apply to loans that are being restructured because of the borrower's default on the original loan?

ANSWER: Yes, assuming that the loan otherwise meets the definition of a "designated loan" and if the lender increases the amount of the loan, or extends or renews the terms of the original loan.

10. A lender makes a loan (not secured by real estate) on the condition that a third party personally guarantees the loan and permits the lender to take a security interest in improved real estate owned by the third party. Is this a "designated loan" to which the regulation applies if the guarantor's property is located in an SFHA in a community that participates in the NFIP?

ANSWER: Yes. The making of a loan on condition of a personal guarantee by a third party and further secured by improved real estate owned by that third party is so closely tied to the making of the loan that it is considered a "designated loan" under the regulation.

II. REQUIREMENT TO PURCHASE FLOOD INSURANCE WHERE AVAILABLE

1. If flood insurance is not available because the community in which the property securing the loan is located in a nonparticipating community in the NFIP, does the regulation apply?

ANSWER: Yes. The regulation still applies, although it does not require the borrower to obtain flood insurance. The lender must make a determination on the Special Flood Hazard Determination Form (SFHDF) to determine whether the property is located in an SFHA and notify the borrower if it is, in fact, located or to be located in an SFHA. The lender may make a conventional loan in an SFHA in a nonparticipating community if the lender chooses to do so. Nevertheless, institutions should exercise good risk management practices to ensure that making loans on properties that are in SFHAs where no flood insurance is available does not create unacceptable risks in an institution's loan portfolio. Government-guaranteed or insured loans (e.g., the Small Business Administration, the Department of Veterans

Affairs and the Federal Housing Administration) are not permitted to be made in nonparticipating communities (see 42 USC 4106(a)).

2. Does the regulation apply to loans purchased from others?

ANSWER: No. The regulation lists certain events that trigger its requirements: making, increasing, extending, or renewing a designated loan. The purchase of a loan is not an event that requires the purchaser to make a new determination at the time of purchase. However, if the lender becomes aware at some point during the life of the loan that flood insurance is required, then the lender must comply with the regulation. Similarly, if the lender extends, increases, or renews the loan, the regulation applies.

3. What about table funding programs? Are they treated as originations or as loans purchased from others?

ANSWER: Loans made through a table funding process will be treated as though the party providing the funds has originated the loan. The funding party must comply with the regulation. The table funding lender can meet the administrative requirements of the regulation by requiring the party processing and underwriting the application to perform those functions on its behalf.

4. How are loans that are now underinsured because of previous insurance limitations to be handled?

ANSWER: In accordance with the act, the Federal Insurance Administration has increased the amount of insurance available under the NFIP. Consequently, loans that previously had principal balances in excess of the program limits may now be underinsured. The new insurance limitations went into effect on March 1, 1995. Lenders and servicers must adjust coverage limits at the first renewal date or the first anniversary date following March 1, 1995, if the policy is a multi-year policy. Loans made on or after March 1, 1995, are subject to the new limits.

5. If the insurable value of the building securing the loan is less than the outstanding balance of the loan, can a lender require the borrower to obtain flood insurance up to the balance of the loan?

ANSWER: No. The insurable value of the improvements to the real estate securing the loan governs the amount of insurance required. The amount of required insurance coverage is the lesser of the principal balance of the loan(s) or the maximum coverage available under the NFIP. An NFIP policy will not provide insurance coverage for losses in excess of the value of the improvements. Since the NFIP policy does not cover land value, lenders should determine the amount of insurance necessary based on the value of the improvements.

6. How do the flood insurance requirements apply in situations involving loan servicing?

Scenario 1 – The loan is originated by a regulated lender and secured by a building on property located in an SFHA in a community in which flood insurance is available under Title V of the Riegle Community Development and Regulatory Improvement Act of 1994. The borrower is provided appropriate notice and insurance is obtained. The lender services the loan. The loan is subsequently sold to a nonregulated party and servicing is transferred to that party. What responsibilities are imposed on the regulated lender? What if the regulated lender only transfers or sells the servicing rights?

ANSWER: The regulated lender must comply with all requirements of the regulation, including making the initial determination, providing appropriate notice to the borrower, and ensuring that the proper amount of insurance is obtained. When the loan is sold and servicing is transferred to the new servicer, the lender must provide notice of the identity of the new servicer to FEMA or its designee.

If the regulated lender retains ownership of the loan and only transfers or sells servicing rights to a nonregulated party, the lender must notify FEMA or its designee, of the identity of the new servicer. The servicing contract should require the servicer to comply with all the requirements that are imposed on the lender as owner of the loan, including escrow of insurance premiums and forced placement (if necessary).

More generally, the regulation does not impose obligations on a loan servicer independent from the obligations it imposes on the owner of a loan. Loan servicers are covered by the escrow, forced placement, and flood hazard determination fee provisions of Title V and regulation primarily to ensure that they may perform the administrative tasks for the lender, without fear of liability to the borrower for imposing unauthorized charges. In addition, the preamble to the regulation emphasizes that the obligation of a loan servicer to fulfill administrative duties with respect to the flood insurance requirements arises from the contractual relationship between the loan servicer and the lender or from other commonly accepted standards for performance of servicing obligations. The lender remains ultimately liable for fulfillment of those responsibilities, and must take adequate steps to ensure that the loan servicer will comply with the flood insurance requirements.

Scenario 2 – The loan is originated by a nonregulated lender. The property is located in an SFHA, but the lender did not make an initial determination or notify the borrower of the need to obtain insurance. The loan is purchased by a regulated lender who also services the loan. What are the responsibilities of the regulated lender? What if the regulated lender purchases only the servicing rights?

ANSWER: If the loan is purchased by the regulated lender, no determination is necessary at that point nor is any notice to FEMA required. If, at some time in the future, the lender becomes aware that the property is located in an

SFHA in a community in which flood insurance is available under the act, it must notify the borrower of that fact and require the borrower to purchase flood insurance. If the borrower does not voluntarily comply, the lender must force place the insurance. If servicing is subsequently sold or transferred, the lender must also notify FEMA or its designee, of the identity of the new servicer.

If the regulated lender purchases only the servicing rights to the loan, the lender is only obligated to follow the terms of its servicing contract with the owner of the loan.

7. A loan is secured by multiple agricultural buildings located throughout a large geographic area. Some of the properties are located in an SFHA and others are not. In addition, the buildings are located in several jurisdictions or counties where some of the communities participate in the NFIP, and others do not. What are the flood insurance requirements for security properties in this scenario?

ANSWER: Flood insurance would be required only on those buildings located in an SFHA in which the community participates in the NFIP. A notice of special flood hazard is required for those buildings located in an SFHA whether or not the community participates in the NFIP. The amount of insurance required will depend upon the principal amount of the loan, the value of the buildings located in participating communities, and the amount of insurance available under the NFIP.

For example, a loan with a principal amount of $150,000 is secured by five buildings, three of which are located in SFHAs within participating communities. The properties are nonresidential in nature; therefore the maximum amount of insurance available under the NFIP is $500,000 per building. Each of the three buildings located in an SFHA must be covered by flood insurance. The total required amount of insurance for the three buildings would be the lesser of $150,000 or the value of the three buildings, with each building insured separately from the others. The amount of required flood insurance could be allocated among the three buildings in varying amounts, so long as each is covered by flood insurance.

8. What is the appropriate amount of coverage under federal flood insurance legislation with respect to residential condominiums, including multi-story condominium complexes?

ANSWER: Effective October 1, 1994, the Federal Insurance Administration issued a new form of master policy for condominiums – the Residential Condominium Building Association Policy (RCBAP). To meet federal flood insurance requirements, an RCBAP should be purchased to cover at least 80 percent of the replacement value of the building or the maximum amount available under the NFIP (currently $250,000 multiplied by the number of units), whichever is less. For instance, the maximum amount of coverage on a 50-unit condominium building would be up to $12.5 million ($250,000 x 50). However, if the replacement value of the building was only $10 million, the condominium association could purchase a policy of $8 million and not be required to have a co-insurance payment in the event of a flood. The $8 million of coverage would meet the requirements of the regulation for all the units within the condominium. A lender should make a similar analysis to determine the amount of coverage for other condominium complexes where flood insurance is required.

When making a loan on a condominium unit located in an SFHA, a lender should determine whether a master policy, or similar product, provides adequate flood insurance coverage and is in place at the time the loan is made. A lender should further ensure that a mechanism is in place (possibly a covenant on the part of the condominium association) that provides for adequate flood insurance coverage for the term of the loan.

9. A lender has a loan secured by a residential condominium unit in a multi-unit complex whose condominium association allows its existing flood insurance policy to lapse. As a result, there is no flood insurance coverage for the condominium unit. What recourse does the lender have?

ANSWER: The NFIP does make individual residential condominium unit policies available (the Dwelling Form) in addition to association master policies. In this instance, the lender, after receiving notice that the association policy has lapsed, must notify the unit owner according to the forced placement procedures to obtain a policy (within 45 days) for the amount of the loan or the maximum amount of coverage available, whichever is less.

III. EXEMPTIONS

1. What are the exemptions from coverage?

ANSWER: There are only two exemptions from the purchase requirements: The first applies to state-owned property covered under a policy of self-insurance satisfactory to the director of FEMA. The second applies if the original principal balance of the loan is $5,000 or less, and the original repayment term is one year or less. Both of these conditions must be present for the second exemption to apply.

IV. ESCROW REQUIREMENTS

1. The effective date of the escrow requirement was October 1, 1996. Does the escrow requirement apply to applications received before October 1, 1996?

ANSWER: The escrow requirement applies only to loans closed on or after October 1, 1996.

2. Are multifamily buildings or mixed-use properties included in the definition of "residential improved real estate"? Are escrows required?

ANSWER: The regulation states that if the collateral securing the loan meets the definition of "residential improved real estate" and the lender requires escrows for other items (e.g., hazard insurance or taxes), then the lender also is required to escrow flood insurance premiums.

Multifamily buildings. Neither Title V of the Riegle Community Development and Regulatory Improvement Act of 1994 nor the regulation distinguishes whether residential improved real estate is single or multifamily, or whether it is owner- or renter-occupied. The preamble to the regulation indicates that single-family dwellings (including mobile homes), two- to four-family dwellings, and multifamily properties containing five or more residential units are covered under the act's escrow provisions. If the building securing the loan meets the regulation's definition of residential improved real estate, and the lender requires the escrow of other items, such as taxes, hazard insurance premiums, etc., then the lender also is required to escrow premiums and fees for flood insurance.

Mixed-use properties. The lender should look to the primary use of a building to determine whether it meets the definition of "residential improved real estate." For example, a building having a retail store on the ground level with a small upstairs apartment used by the store's owner is generally considered a commercial enterprise and consequently would not constitute a residential building under the definition. Even though the regulation does not require escrows for flood insurance, the lender may impose such a requirement through contract.

On the other hand, if the primary use of a mixed-use property is for residential purposes, the regulation's escrow requirements would apply.

3. When must escrow accounts established for flood insurance purposes be administered in accordance with the escrow rules under section 10 of RESPA?

ANSWER: Lenders should look to the definition of "federally related mortgage loan" contained in RESPA to see whether a particular loan is subject to Section 10. Generally, only loans on one- to four-family dwellings will be subject to the escrow requirements of RESPA. Consequently, only those escrow accounts established for loans subject to RESPA are required to conform with section 10 of RESPA. Loans on multifamily dwellings with five or more units are not covered by RESPA requirements.

Pursuant to the regulation, however, lenders must escrow premiums and fees for any required flood insurance if the lender requires escrows for other purposes, such as hazard insurance or taxes. This requirement pertains to any loan, including both those subject to RESPA and those not subject to RESPA. The preceding paragraph addresses the requirement for administering loans covered by RESPA. The preamble to the regulation contains a more detailed discussion of the escrow requirements.

4. Do voluntary escrow accounts, established at the request of the borrower, trigger a requirement for the lender to escrow premiums for required flood insurance?

ANSWER: No. If escrow accounts for other purposes are established at the voluntary request of the borrower, the lender is not required to establish escrow accounts for flood insurance premiums. Examiners should review the loan policies of the lender and the underlying legal obligation between the parties to the loan to determine whether the accounts are, in fact, voluntary. For example, if the loan policies of the lending institution require borrowers to establish escrow accounts for other purposes and the contractual obligation permits the lender to establish escrow accounts for those other purposes, the lender will have the burden of demonstrating that an existing escrow was made pursuant to a voluntary request.

5. Will premiums paid for credit life insurance, disability insurance, or similar voluntary insurance programs be viewed as escrow accounts requiring the escrow of flood insurance premiums?

ANSWER: No. Premiums paid for these types of insurance policies will not trigger the escrow requirement for flood insurance premiums if purchase of these policies is voluntary to the borrower.

6. Will escrow-type accounts for multifamily building commercial loans trigger the escrow requirement for flood insurance premiums?

ANSWER: Various types of accounts are established in connection with commercial-purpose real estate loans. These loans typically involve multifamily properties and are substantially different in purpose and type from escrow accounts on single-family residences. These involve accounts such as "interest reserve accounts," "compensating balance accounts," "marketing accounts," and similar accounts that may be established by contract between the purchaser and seller of the building (although administered by the lender in some cases). Accounts such as these, established in connection with the underlying agreement between the buyer and seller, or that relate to the commercial venture itself, do not constitute escrow accounts for the purpose of the regulation. Escrow accounts for the protection of the property, such as escrows for hazard insurance premiums or local real estate taxes, are the types of escrow accounts that trigger the requirement to escrow flood insurance premiums.

7. What requirements for escrow accounts apply to properties covered by Residential Condominium Building Association Policies (RCBAP)?

ANSWER: RCBAPs are policies purchased by a condominium association on behalf of the individual unit owners in the condominium. The premiums on the policy are paid by a portion of the periodic dues paid to the association by the condominium owners. When a lender makes a loan to purchase a condominium over which an RCBAP is in place and the premiums are paid by dues to the condominium association, the escrow requirement is satisfied. Lenders should exercise due diligence with respect to continuing compliance with the insurance requirements on the part of the condominium association.

V. REQUIRED USE OF STANDARD FLOOD HAZARD DETERMINATION FORM

1. Does the SFHDF replace the current borrower notification form?

ANSWER: No. The notification form is used to notify the borrower(s) that they are purchasing improved property located in an SFHA. The financial regulatory agencies, in consultation with FEMA, included a revised version of the sample borrower notification form in appendix A to the regulation. The SFHDF is used by the lender to determine whether the property securing the loan is located in an SFHA.

2. Must the SFHDF be provided to the borrower? If so, must the borrower sign the form acknowledging receipt?

ANSWER: Although it may be a common practice in some areas for lenders to provide a copy of the SFHDF to the borrower to give to the insurance agent, lenders are neither required nor prohibited from providing the borrower with a copy of the form. The signature of the borrower is not required on the SFHDF.

3. May the SFHDF be used in electronic format?

ANSWER: Yes. FEMA, in the final rule adopting the SFHDF, stated: "If an electronic format is used, the format and exact layout of the Standard Flood Hazard Determination Form is not required, but the fields and elements listed on the form are required. Any electronic format used by lenders must contain all mandatory fields indicated on the form." It should be noted, however, that the lender must be able to reproduce the form upon receiving a document request by its federal supervisory agency.

4. Section 528 of the Riegle Community Development and Regulatory Improvement Act of 1994 permits a lender to rely on a previous determination using the SFHDF when it is increasing, extending, renewing, or purchasing a loan secured by a building or a mobile home. The act omits the "making" of a loan as a permissible event to rely on a previous determination. May a lender rely on a previous determination for a refinancing or assumption of a loan?

ANSWER: It depends. If a subsequent loan involving a refinancing or assumption is made on the same property by the same lender that obtained the original determination, and the other requirements contained in Section 528 are met, the lender may rely on the previous determination. Section 528 of the act states that a lender may rely on a previous determination only if the original determination was recorded on the SFHDF within the previous seven years and if there were no map revisions or updates affecting the security property since the original determination was made. However, a loan refinancing or assumption made by a lender other than the lender who obtained the original determination would constitute a new loan, thereby requiring a new determination.

5. If a borrower requesting a home equity loan secured by a junior lien provides evidence that flood insurance coverage is in place, does the lender have to make a new determination? Does the lender have to adjust the amount of the insurance coverage?

ANSWER: It depends. Assuming the requirements of Section 528 are met and the lender made the first mortgage, then a new determination would not be necessary. If, however, a lender other than the one who made the first mortgage loan is making the home equity loan, a new determination would be required because this lender would be deemed to be "making" a new loan. In any event, the institution will need to determine whether the amount of insurance in force is sufficient to cover either the principal balance of all loans (including the home equity loan) or the maximum amount of coverage available on the improved real estate, whichever is less.

VI. FORCED PLACEMENT OF FLOOD INSURANCE

1. Is forced placement allowed? What are the procedures?

ANSWER: Title V and the regulation require a lender to force place flood insurance if all of the following circumstances occur:

- The lender determines at any time during the life of the loan that the property securing the loan is located in an SFHA;
- The community in which the property is located participates in the NFIP;
- Flood insurance coverage is inadequate or does not exist; and
- The borrower fails to purchase the appropriate amount of coverage.

To force place, a lender must notify the borrower of the required amount of flood insurance that must be obtained within 45 days after notification. The notice also must state that if the borrower does not obtain the insurance within the 45-day period, the lender will purchase the insurance on behalf of the borrower and may charge the borrower the cost of premiums and fees to obtain the coverage. (Standard FNMA/FHLMC documents permit the servicer or lender to add those charges to the principal amount of the loan.)

FEMA developed the Mortgage Portfolio Protection Program (MPPP) to assist lenders in connection with forced placement procedures. FEMA published these procedures in the Federal Register on August 29, 1995 (60 FR 44881). Appendix A to the regulation contains examples of notification letters to be used in connection with the MPPP.

2. Can a servicer force place on behalf of a lender?

ANSWER: Yes. Assuming the statutory prerequisites for forced placement are met, and subject to the servicing contract between the lender and the servicer, the act clearly authorizes servicers to force place flood insurance on behalf of the lender, following the procedures set forth in the regulation.

3. When forced placement occurs, what is the amount of insurance required to be placed?

ANSWER: The amount of flood insurance coverage required is the same regardless of how the insurance is placed. (See Section II, Requirement to Purchase Flood Insurance Where Available.)

VII. DETERMINATION FEES

1. When can lenders or servicers charge the borrower a fee for making a determination?

ANSWER: There are four instances under Title V and regulation when the borrower can be charged a specific fee for a flood determination:

- When the determination is made in connection with the making, increasing, extending, or renewing of a loan initiated by the borrower.

- When the determination is prompted by a revision or update of floodplain areas or flood-risk zones by FEMA.

- When the determination is prompted by FEMA's publication of a notice or compendia that affects the area in which the security property is located.

- When the determination results in forced placement of insurance.

Loan or other contractual documents between the parties may also permit the imposition of fees.

2. May charges made for life-of-loan reviews by flood determination firms be passed along to the borrower?

ANSWER: Yes. Many flood determination firms serve lenders by conducting periodic reviews of loans to ascertain whether the original determinations remain valid. This service is sometimes coupled with the original determination. The fee charged is thus a composite one for conducting both the original and subsequent reviews. Charging a fee for the original determination is clearly within the permissible purposes envisioned by the act. The agencies agree that a determination fee may include, among other things, reasonable fees for a lender, servicer, or third party to monitor the flood hazard status of property securing a loan to make determinations on an ongoing basis.

Consequently, the agencies also believe that a fee for life-of-loan service may be passed along to the borrower. However, because the life-of-loan fee is based on the ability to charge a determination fee, the monitoring fee may be charged only if the events specified in the answer to question VII. 1 occur.

VIII. NOTICE OF SPECIAL FLOOD HAZARDS AND AVAILABILITY OF FEDERAL DISASTER RELIEF

1. Does the notice have to be provided to each applicant for a real estate related loan?

ANSWER: The notice must be provided to borrowers only when the lender determines that the property securing the loan is or will be located in an SFHA. In a transaction involving multiple borrowers, the agencies believe it is only necessary to provide the notice to any one of the borrowers in the transaction. Lenders may provide multiple notices if they choose. The lender and borrower(s) typically designate the borrower to whom the notice will be provided.

2. Lenders making loans on mobile homes may not always know where the home is to be located until just prior to, or sometimes after, the time of loan closing. How is the notice requirement applied in these situations?

ANSWER: In mobile home transactions, lenders can meet the notice requirement by providing notice to the borrower as soon as practicable after determining that the mobile home will be located in an SFHA and, if possible, before completing the loan transaction. In circumstances where time constraints can be anticipated, regulated lenders should use their best efforts to provide adequate notice of flood hazards to borrowers at the earliest possible time.

When loans are secured by mobile homes not located on a permanent foundation, the agencies note that such "home only" mobile home transactions are excluded from the definition of mobile home and the notice requirements would not apply to these transactions. However, as indicated in the preamble to the regulation, the agencies encourage a lender to advise the borrower that if the mobile home is later located on a permanent foundation in an SFHA, flood insurance may be required. If the lender, when notified of the location of the mobile home subsequent to the loan closing, determines that it has been placed on a permanent foundation and is located in an SFHA in which flood insurance is available under the act, flood insurance coverage becomes mandatory and appropriate notice must be given to the borrower under those provisions. If the borrower fails to purchase flood insurance coverage within 45 days after notification, the lender must force place the insurance.

3. When is the lender required to provide notice to the servicer of a loan that flood insurance is required?

ANSWER: Because the loan servicer is often not identified before the loan closing, the regulation requires that notice be provided no later than the time the lender transmits other loan data, such as information concerning hazard insurance and taxes, to the servicer.

4. What will constitute an appropriate form of notice to the servicer?

ANSWER: Delivery to the servicer of a copy of the notice given to the borrower is appropriate notice. The regulation also provides that the notice can be made either electronically or by a written copy.

5. In the case of a servicer affiliated with the lender, is it necessary to provide the notice?

ANSWER: Yes. Title V requires the lender to notify the servicer of special flood hazards and the regulation reflects this requirement. Neither contains an exception for affiliates.

6. How long does the lender have to maintain the borrower's record of receipt of the notice?

ANSWER: The borrower's record of receipt of the notice must be maintained for the time that the lender owns the loan. Lenders may keep the record in the form that best suits the lender's business practices. Lenders may retain the record electronically, but they must be able to retrieve the record within a reasonable time pursuant to a document request from their federal supervisory agency.

IX. NOTICE OF SERVICER'S IDENTITY

1. When a lender makes a designated loan and the lender will be servicing that loan, what are the requirements for notifying the director of FEMA or the director's designee?

ANSWER: FEMA stated in a June 4, 1996, letter that the director's designee is the insurance company issuing the flood insurance policy. The borrower's purchase of a policy (or the lender's forced placement of a policy), will constitute notice to FEMA when the lender is servicing that loan. In the event the servicing subsequently is transferred to a new servicer, the lender must provide notice to the insurance company of the identity of the new servicer.

2. Would a RESPA notice of transfer sent to the director of FEMA (or the director's designee) satisfy the regulatory provisions of the act?

ANSWER: Delivery of a copy of the notice of transfer or any other form of notice is sufficient if the sender includes, on or with the notice, the following information:

- Borrower's full name,
- Flood insurance policy number,

- Property address (including city and state),
- Name of bank or servicer making notification,
- Name and address of new servicer, and
- Name and telephone number of contact person at new servicer.

3. Can delivery of the notice be made electronically, including batch transmissions?

ANSWER: Yes. The regulation specifically permits transmission by electronic means and a timely batch transmission of the notice also would be permissible, if it is acceptable to the director's designee.

4. If the loan and its servicing rights are sold by the lender, is the lender required to provide notice to the director or the director's designee?

ANSWER: Yes. Failure to provide such notice would defeat the purpose of the notice requirement because FEMA would have no record of the identity of either the owner or servicer of the loan.

5. Is the lender required to provide notice when a servicer other than the lender sells or transfers the servicing rights to another servicer?

ANSWER: No. The obligation of the lender to notify the director or the director's designee of the identity of the servicer transfers to the new servicer. The duty to notify the director or the director's designee of any subsequent sale or transfer of the servicing rights and responsibilities belongs to that servicer. For example, First Financial Institution makes and services the loan. It then sells the loan in the secondary market and also sells the servicing rights to First Financial Mortgage Company. First Financial Institution notifies the director's designee of the identity of the new servicer and the other information requested by FEMA so that FEMA can track the loan. If First Financial Mortgage Company later sells the servicing rights to another firm, First Financial Mortgage Company is responsible for notifying the director's designee of the identity of the new servicer, not First Financial Institution.

6. In the event of a merger of one lending institution with another, what are the responsibilities of the parties for notifying the director's designee?

ANSWER: If an institution is acquired by or merges with another institution, the duty to provide notice for the loans being serviced by the acquired institution will fall to the successor institution in the event that notification is not provided by the acquired institution prior to the effective date of the acquisition or merger.

X.   12 CFR 22, APPENDIX A – SAMPLE FORM OF NOTICE OF SPECIAL FLOOD HAZARDS AND AVAILABILITY OF FEDERAL DISASTER RELIEF ASSISTANCE

1. Is use of the sample form of notice mandatory? Can it be revised to accommodate a lender's needs?

ANSWER: Although lenders are required to provide notice to a borrower purchasing property secured by an improved structure located in an SFHA, use of the sample form of notice provided in appendix A to the regulation is not mandatory. It should be noted that the sample form includes other information in addition to what is required by Title V and the regulation. Lenders may personalize, change the format, and add information to the sample form if they choose. However, a lender-revised form must provide the borrower with at least the minimum information required by the regulation. Therefore, lenders should consult the regulation to determine the information needed.

National Flood Insurance Program Regional Offices

NFIP offices are field offices of the Federal Insurance Administration's servicing contractor for the National Flood Insurance Program. Specific questions regarding the NFIP may be directed to the appropriate office.

Region I
140 Wood Road
Suite 200
Braintree, Massachusetts 02184
(781) 848-1908
(CT, MA, ME, NH, RI, VT)

Region II
33 Wood Avenue, South
Suite 600
Iselin, New Jersey 08830
(732) 603-3875
(NJ, NY)

Caribbean Area Office
1407 J. T. Pinero
Caparra Terrace, Puerto Rico 00921
(787) 782-2733
(Puerto Rico, and the Virgin Islands)

Region III
1930 East Marlton Pike
Building T, Suite 9
Cherry Hill, New Jersey 08003-4219
(609) 489-4003
(DC, DE, MD, PA, VA, WV)

Region IV
1532 Dunwoody Village Parkway
Suite 200
Dunwoody, Georgia 30338
(770) 396-9117
(AL, FL, GA, KY, MS, NC, SC, TN)

Region V
1111 East Warrenville Road
Suite 209
Naperville, Illinois 60563
(630) 577-1407
(IL, IN, MI, MN, OH, WI)

Region VI
11931 Wickchester Road
Suite 304
Houston, Texas 77043
(281) 531-5990
(AR, LA, NM, OK, TX)

Region VII
The Courtyard
601 N. Mur-Len Road
Suite 13-B
Olathe, Kansas 66062-5445
(913) 780-4238 or (913) 780-4247
(IA, KS, MO, NE)

Region VIII
2801 Youngfield Street
Suite 300
Golden, Colorado 80401
(303) 275-3475
(CO, MT, ND, SD, UT, WY)

Region IX
5777 Madison Avenue
Suite 810
Sacramento, California 95841
(916) 334-1720
(AZ, CA, Guam, HI, NV)

Region X
1611 116th Avenue, NE
Suite 116
Bellevue, Washington 98004
(425) 646-4908
(AK, ID, OR, WA)

NFIP Information

NUMBER	LOCATION	SERVICE
800-427-4661	Telephone Response Center	NFIP Questions
800-611-6125	Telephone Response Center	Lender Questions
800-358-9616	Map Service Center	Community status information & maps

INTERNET

http://www.fema.gov/	FEMA's Home Page
http://www.fema.gov/library/sfldfrm.pdf	Standard Flood Hazard Determination Form
http://www.fema.gov/fema/csb.htm	Community status information

NFIP MATERIALS AND RELATED FORMS

Mandatory Purchase of Flood Insurance Guidelines, revised 5/97 (FEMA-186). This booklet is available on the Internet Web site http://www.fema.gov/nfip/mpurfi.htm.

Answers to Questions About the National Flood Insurance Program, revised 11/97 (FIA-2). This booklet is available on the Internet Web site http://www.fema.gov/nfip/q&a.pdf.

To obtain a copy of these publications and other NFIP materials and forms, you may write or phone your request to:

FEMA Distribution Facility
P.O. Box 2012
Jessup, MD 20794-2012
Telephone: 800-480-2520
Fax: 301-362-5335

To obtain copies of flood maps or Standard Flood Hazard Determination Forms, you may write to: Federal Emergency Management Agency, Map Service Center, 6730 Santa Barbara Court, Baltimore, MD 21227-5624.

Glossary of Terms

Base Flood Elevation – The elevation shown on the Flood Insurance Rate Map (FIRM) for Zones AE, AH, A1-A30, AR, AR/A1-30, AR/AE, AR/AO, AR/AA, V1-V30, and VE that indicates the water surface elevation resulting from a flood that has a one-percent chance of equaling or exceeding that level in any given year.

Designated Loan – A loan secured by a building or mobile home that is located or to be located in a special flood hazard area in which flood insurance is available under the National Flood Insurance Program.

Emergency Program – Typically the first phase under which a community participates in the National Flood Insurance Program. It is intended to provide a limited amount of insurance coverage at subsidized rates to all insurable structures in that community before the effective date of the initial Flood Insurance Rate Map.

Evidence of Insurance – The National Flood Insurance Program does not recognize an oral binder or contract of insurance. A copy of the flood insurance application, premium payment, and declarations page submitted to the lender is sufficient evidence of proof of purchase.

Flood Hazard Boundary Map (FHBM) – Official map of a community on which the approximate boundaries of the flood, mudslide, and related erosion areas with special hazards have been designated.

Flood Insurance Rate Map (FIRM) – Official map of a community delineating both the special hazard areas and the risk premium zones applicable to the community. These maps are more detailed than boundary maps.

Floodplain – Any land area susceptible to being inundated by flood waters from any source.

Flood Zone – Zones that begin with the letters V and A are Special Flood Hazard Areas (SFHAs). Zones B, C, D, or X are moderate/minimal flood hazard areas in which flood insurance is not required by law but is recommended.

Letter of Map Amendment (LOMA) – An amendment to the map currently in effect, which establishes that a property is not located in a Special Flood Hazard Area (SFHA). A LOMA may be necessary because a flood map does not reflect a rise in terrain that is inadvertently included in the SFHA. A property owner can submit elevation materials in support of a request for a

LOMA to remove a property from the SFHA. There is no requirement that the community or lender become involved. Only FEMA can issue a LOMA.

Letter of Map Revision (LOMR) – An official amendment to the map currently in effect. It is issued by FEMA and changes flood zones, delineations and elevations. A LOMR may be issued, for example, when a property owner grades and fills the site to raise the level of the land above the 100-year flood level. A request for a LOMR requires concurrence of the community. Only FEMA can revise a map by a LOMR.

Mortgage Portfolio Protection Program (MPPP) – A program for forced placement of flood insurance designed to help lending institutions maintain compliance with the FDPA. Policies written under the MPPP can be placed only through a Write Your Own Company.

National Flood Insurance Program (NFIP) – A program that makes flood insurance available on a nationwide basis through the cooperative efforts of the federal government and the private insurance industry and that encourages state and local governments to exercise sound floodplain management to reduce losses caused by flood.

Nonparticipating Community – A community for which the Federal Insurance Administration has not authorized the sale of flood insurance under the National Flood Insurance Program.

One Hundred Year Flood – Any flood zone that begins with the letter A or V is designated as having a flood level with a 1 percent or greater chance of being flooded in any year. These high-risk zones are also known as Special Flood Hazard Areas (SFHAs). Over the life of a 30-year loan, there is a 26 percent chance of experiencing a flood within an SFHA.

Participating Community – A community for which the Federal Insurance Administration has authorized the sale of flood insurance under the National Flood Insurance Program.

Regular Program – The phase of a community's participation in the National Flood Insurance Program (NFIP) in which more comprehensive floodplain management requirements are imposed and higher amounts of insurance are available based upon risk zones and elevations determined in a flood insurance study. The Flood Insurance Rate Map (FIRM) is the map used in this phase of the NFIP.

Remapping – FEMA reviews the maps every five years to keep abreast of the natural changes in flood plains. The results of FEMA's remapped territories are published regularly in a six-month compendium in the Federal Register.

Standard Flood Hazard Determination Form (SFHDF) – FEMA's form 81-93, effective January 2, 1996, must be used by all companies performing determinations. The form may be in a printed, computerized, or electronic format. A completed form must be maintained for every loan secured by improved real estate.

Special Flood Hazard Area (SFHA) – The area on an FHBM or FIRM that has a 1 percent or greater chance of being flooded in any year. SFHAs are coded as Zones A, AO, AH, A1-A30, AE, A99, AR, AR/A, AR/AE, AR/A1-A30, AR/AH, AR/AO, V, V1-V30, and VE and are darkly shaded on the FIRM.

Write Your Own (WYO) Program – A cooperative undertaking between the insurance industry and the Federal Insurance Administration. The WYO Program operates within the context of the National Flood Insurance Program (NFIP) and involves private insurance carriers that issue and service NFIP policies.

Laws

    42 USC 4001 et seq., Flood Disaster Protection Act

Regulations

    12 CFR 22, Loans in Areas Having Special Flood Hazards